Phonics Success

sleeping

row a boat

one fox
a family of foxes

Louis Fidge and Christine Moorcroft

Contents

4-5   **Introduction**

Spelling vowel sounds
6-7   Sounds like ay
8-9   Sounds like igh
10-11   Sounds like oo
12-13   Sounds like oh
14-15   Sounds like ow
16-17   Sounds like uh
18-19   Sounds like ar
20   y or ey
21   ee or ea
22   au or aw
23   or or oar
24-25   Sounds like ay
26   Words with ie
27   Words with oe
28   oy or oi
29   air or are
30-31   Sounds like ur

Spelling consonant sounds
32-33   Sounds like ch
34-35   When le says l
36-37   When st says s
38-39   Sounds like sh
40-41   z or s
42   When gh says f
43   When sc says s

Suffixes
44-45   Suffix –ed (1)
46-47   Suffix –ed (2)
48-49   Suffix –ed (3)
50-51   Suffix –ing (1)
52-53   Suffix –ing (2)
54-55   Suffix –ing (3)

56–57	Suffix –s
58–59	Suffix –es
60–61	Suffix –er (1)
62–63	Suffix –er (2)
64–65	Suffix –er (3)
66–67	Suffix –est (1)
68–69	Suffix –est (2)
70–71	Suffix –est (3)
72–73	Suffix –ful
74–75	Suffix –ly (1)
76–77	Suffix –ly (2)
78–79	Suffix –y

Prefixes
80–81	Prefix un–
82–83	Prefix dis–
84–85	Prefix re–

Spelling strategies
86	Syllables
87	Look-alike, sound-alike words
88–89	Compound words (1)
90–91	Compound words (2)
92–93	Clues for tricky words
94	Remembering tricky words

What have I learned?
95–96	What have I learned?

Introduction

What is phonics?

Phonics is the relationship between sounds (phonemes) and letters or groups of letters (graphemes). Learning phonics involves listening to sounds, recognising sounds, discriminating between sounds, and learning how sounds are represented by letters.

Phonics Practice Activities 3 is based on current practice in schools and presents letters and sounds in ways that should be familiar to learners from their school work. This book will support teachers in helping the learners to improve their reading and spelling using phonics.

Phonics for children (ages 6 to 7)

The learners can use phonics to help them to read words they do not know. In fact, their phonic knowledge is sometimes tested in this way - reading 'pseudo' words using phonics alone. However, when learners encounter words in a piece of text the context helps. This is useful when they are faced with words that could be pronounced in more than one way. Teachers are encouraged to explain any new words in order to develop their the learner's vocabulary.

This book builds on learners' previous learning (see *Phonics Practice Activities 1* and *2*). It introduces a number of new sounds and the letters that can represent them, including...

- different ways of spelling sounds learners have already learned
- alternative pronunciations for letters or combinations of letters
- adding prefixes to change the meanings of words
- adding suffixes to form plurals, past tenses and different forms of adjectives and verbs.

In addition to learning phonics, learners should have opportunities to read as many different types of text as possible for pleasure and for information, as well as reading texts that warn or advise. The learners should have opportunities to explore sounds and make up rhymes – however silly!

This book helps learners to learn the relationship between sounds and letters. They will learn:

- Alternative spellings for vowel sounds, including those that are spelled using more than one letter.
- Alternative spellings for consonant sounds, including unusual ones such as gh for 'f' and sc or st for 's'.
- Different sounds represented by the same letters.
- Adding suffixes to change the meanings of words and the different sounds produced by the suffix -ed.
- Adding prefixes to change the meanings of words.
- Spelling strategies for difficult words.

How this book is organised

Spelling vowel sounds (pages 6–31) further develops learners' knowledge of the different ways of spelling vowel sounds: 'ay' (ai, ay, eigh), 'igh' (y, igh, i–e, ie), 'oo' (oo, ew, u–e), 'oh' (oa, ow, o–e, oe), 'ow' (ow, ou), 'uh' (er, our), 'ar' (a, al), 'ee' (y, ey, ee, ea), 'or' (aw, au, or, oar), 'oy' (oi, oy), 'air' (air, are), 'ur' (ur, ear, or).

Spelling consonant sounds (pages 32–43) further develops learners' knowledge of the different ways of spelling consonant sounds: 'ch' (ch, tch, t), 'l' (l, le), 's' (st, sc), 'sh' (ch, ci, ti, ssi), 'z' (z, s), 'f' (gh).

Suffixes (pages 44–79) helps to develop an understanding of how suffixes change the meanings and spellings of words. This section helps develop an understanding of spelling patterns for words where suffixes are added: -ed, -s, -es, -er, -est, -ful, -ly, -y.

Prefixes (pages 80–85) introduces simple prefixes that change the spelling and meaning of a word: un-, dis-, re-.

Spelling strategies (pages 86–94) helps learners develop strategies to help them make the correct choices for spelling difficult words:

- Splitting longer words into syllables
- Noticing spelling patterns such as 'ould' in would and could
- Combining words to create compound words
- Using clues to help with difficult words such as friend, busy, cupboard
- Using quirky or funny mnemonics to help learners remember tricky words such as beauty, equal, cycle.

What have I learned?

This section provides activities to help the learners assess what has been learned. It helps you to determine what further practice the learner needs.

Sounds like ay

tray

chain

gate

Read the rhyme

Colour the letters that say **ay**:   ay   ai   a-e

Today it may rain

So I shall take the train.

There was no long wait

So I shall not be late.

Teacher's tip

Begin by reading the rhyme to the learner and asking him/her which sound they hear often. Ask the learner to write the letters that stand for the 'ay' sound. Then show the pictures and words at the top of the page and read them aloud. Point out the different letters that can be used to write this sound. The learner could then follow the rhyme on the page as you read it with him/her.

Read and match the words

Read the words. Listen to the **ay** sound.

Look at the letters. Colour the letters that say **ay**.

Match the words to the ones in the chart.

Write the words below.

tray	chain	gate

Sounds like igh

sky

high

kite

Read the rhyme

Colour the letters that say **igh**: y   igh   i-e

If I could fly high up in the sky
Like a kite in the night.
I think I might fly
Right out of sight.

Teacher's tip

Begin by reading the rhyme to the learner and asking him/her which sound they hear often. Ask the learner to write the letters that stand for the 'igh' sound. Then show the pictures and words at the top of the page and read them aloud. Point out the different letters that can be used to write this sound. The learner could then follow the rhyme on the page as you read it with him/her.

Read and match the words

Read the words. Listen to the **igh** sound.

Look at the letters. Colour the letters that say **igh**.

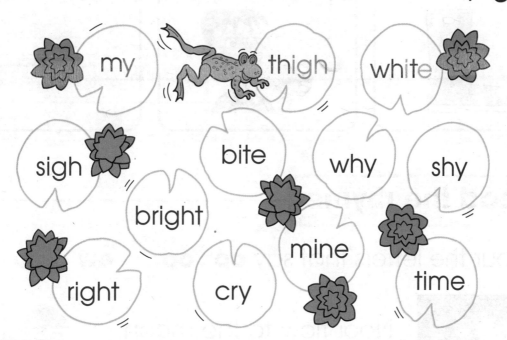

my   thigh   white

sigh   bite   why   shy

bright   mine

right   cry   time

Match the words to the ones in the chart.

Write the words below.

sky	high	kite

Sounds like oo

boot
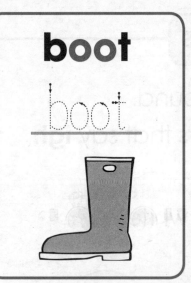

chew

ruler

Read the rhyme

Colour the letters that say **oo**: **oo**   **ew**   **u-e**

Noor flew to the moon.
Roop drew a spoon.

Bruno, in a bad mood,
threw some food.

But what about June?
She got her flute and
played a tune.

Read and match the words

Read the words. Listen to the **oo** sound.

Look at the letters. Colour the letters that say **oo**.

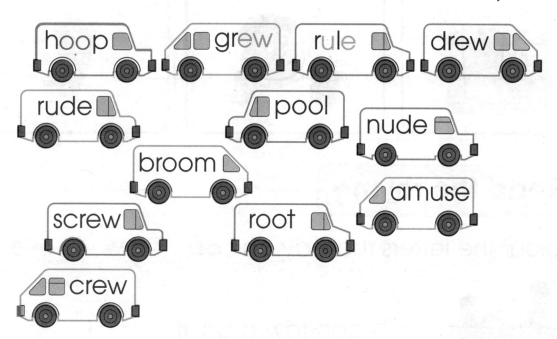

Match the words to the ones in the chart.

Write the words below.

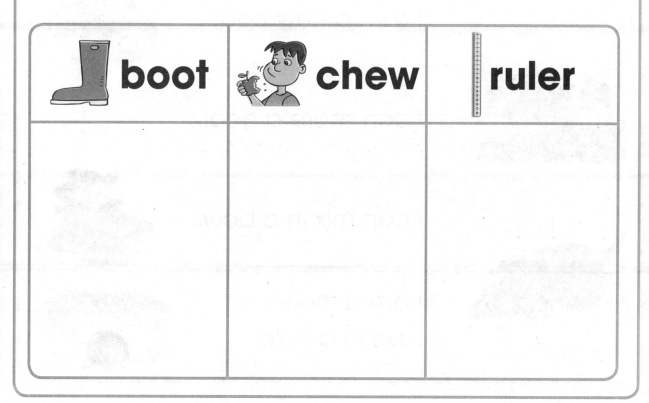

boot	chew	ruler

Sounds like oh

road

road

blow

blow

cone

cone

Read the rhyme

Colour the letters that say **oh**: **oa**   **ow**   **o-e**

I can row a boat.

I own a new coat.

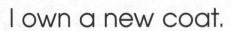

I can score a goal.

I can mix in a bowl.

I am a mole.
I live in a hole.

Read and match the words

Read the words. Listen to the **oh** sound.

Look at the letters. Colour the letters that say **oh**.

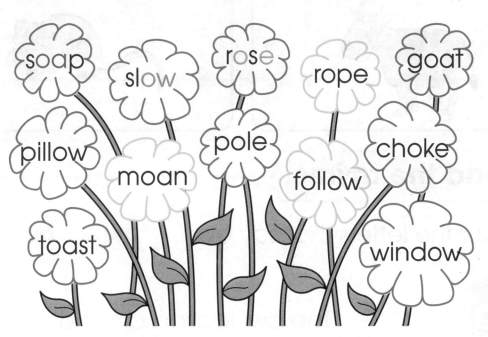

Match the words to the ones in the chart.

Write the words below.

🏞️ **road**	😗 **blow**	🍦 **cone**

Sounds like ow

cow

cow

mouse

mouse

Read the rhyme

Colour the letters that say **ow**:   ow   ou

The owl looked around
And came down to the ground.

The old white mouse
Came out of its house.

And a heavy shower
Soaked the flower.

Teacher's tip

Begin by reading the rhyme to the learner and asking him/her which sound they hear often. Ask the learner to write the letters that stand for the 'ow' sound. Then show the pictures and words at the top of the page and read them aloud. Point out the different letters that can be used to write this sound. The learner could then follow the rhyme on the page as you read it with him/her.

Read and match the words

Read the words. Listen to the **ow** sound.

Look at the letters. Colour the letters that say **ow**.

now shout round town

about scowl found crowd

cloud house drown towel

Match the words to the ones in the chart.

Write the words below.

 **cow**	**mouse**

Sounds like uh

hanger

hanger

armour

armour

Read the rhyme

Colour the letters that say **uh**: er   our

Mr Winner has his dinner.

It's not a dinner to make him thinner.

Lots of chips and fish in batter.

Is going to make him fatter.

He eats without a quaver

And says, "I love the flavour."

Read and match the words

Read the words. Listen to the **uh** sound.

Look at the letters. Colour the letters that say **uh**.

scatter · colour · favour · batter

ladder · harbour · father · paper

flavour · winter · neighbour · letter

Match the words to the ones in the chart.

Write the words below.

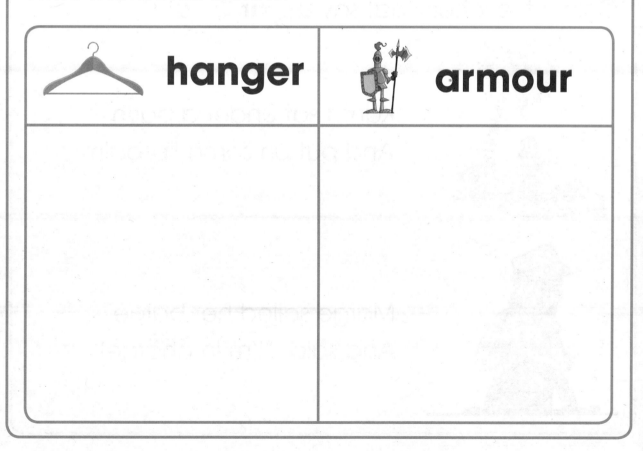

hanger	armour

Sounds like ar

shark

shark

palm

palm

Read the rhyme

Colour the letters that say **ar**: **ar**   **al**

Kanta sat under a palm
And put on some lip-balm.

Marge sailed her barge
And said, "I'm in charge!"

Read and match the words

Read the words. Listen to the **ar** sound.
Look at the letters. Colour the letters that say **ar**.

mark   calm   carpet   spark

calf   party   target   half

starve   calves   charming   parcel

Match the words to the ones in the chart.
Write the words below.

🦈 shark	🌴 palm

y or ey

cherry

cherry

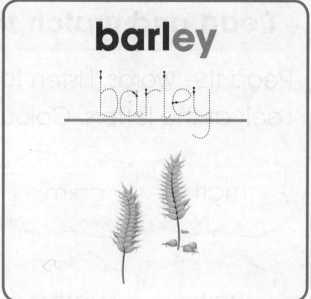

barley

barley

Write the words

Read the words.

baby money key honey turkey donkey

Write the words for the pictures.

_____

_____

_____

_____

_____

_____

Read and sort the words

Read the words. Colour **ee** or **ea**.

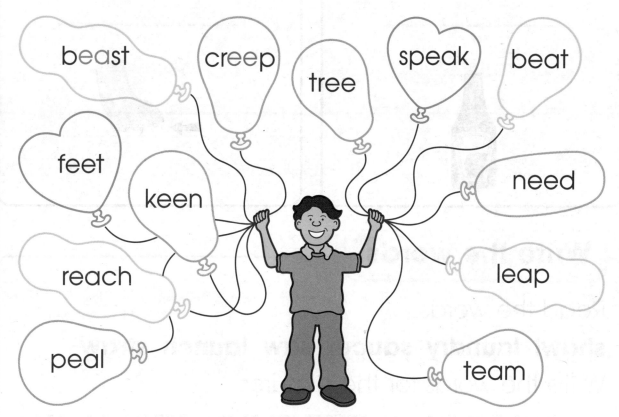

beast   creep   tree   speak   beat

feet   keen   need

reach   leap

peal   team

Sort the words into sets.

ee words	**ea** words

Spelling vowel sounds

sauce

claws

claws

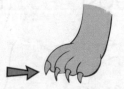

Write the words

Read the words.

shawl laundry saucer saw launch straw

Write the words for the pictures.

morning

morning

roar

roar

Write the words

Read the words.

oar storm whiteboard corn thorn chessboard

Write the words for the pictures.

_____

_____

_____

_____

_____

_____

23

Sounds like ay

reins

hey

Hey!

neigh

Neigh

Read the rhyme

Colour the letters that say **ay**:   ei   ey   eigh

Hey! Neighbours! Hey! Mr Grey!
Santa Claus is here on his sleigh!
Count the reindeer – one, two,
   three, four, five, six, seven, eight!
Pulling, pulling that heavy weight.

Teacher's tip

Begin by reading the rhyme to the learner and asking him/her which sound they hear often. Ask the learner to write the letters that stand for the 'ay' sound. Then show the pictures and words at the top of the page and read them aloud. Point out the different letters that can be used to write this sound. The learner could then follow the rhyme on the page as you read it with him/her. After completing this page, return to p.6 and remind the learner of the other letters that can be used to spell the 'ay' sound.

Sounds like ay

Read and match the words

Read the words. Listen to the **ay** sound.

Look at the letters. Colour the letters that say **ay**.

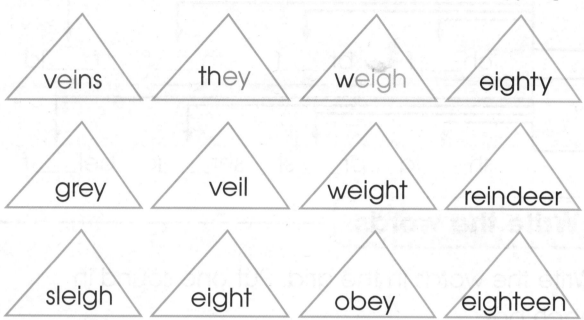

veins   they   weigh   eighty

grey   veil   weight   reindeer

sleigh   eight   obey   eighteen

Match the words to the ones in the chart.

Write the words below.

reins	hey	neigh

Words with ie

Make the words

Make some words with **ie**. Read the words.

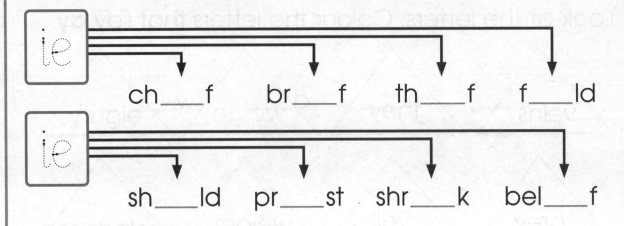

| ie |

ch___f   br___f   th___f   f___ld

| ie |

sh___ld   pr___st   shr___k   bel___f

Write the words

Write the words in the grid. Put one sound in each box.

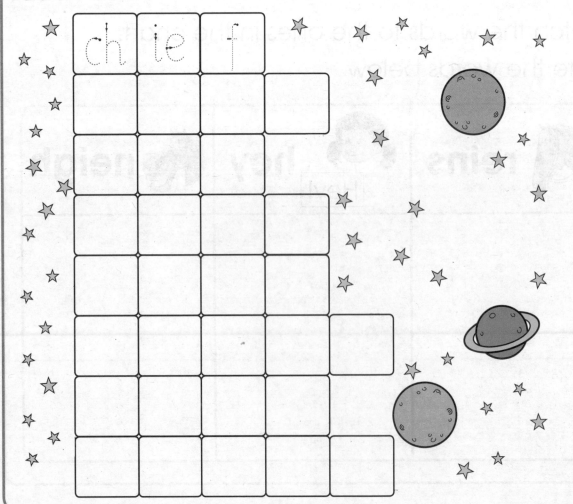

Make the words

Make some words with **oe**. Read the words.

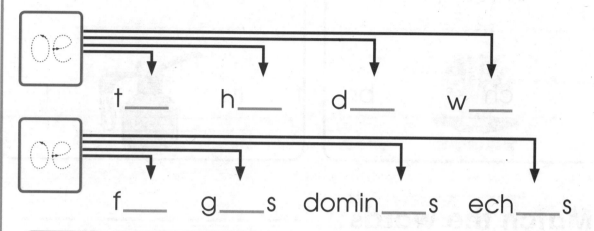

t___   h___   d___   w___

f___   g___s   domin___s   ech___s

Write the words

Write the words in the grid. Put one sound in each box.

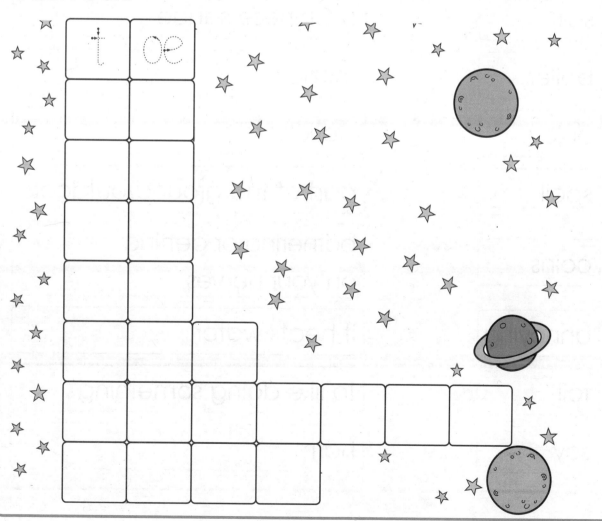

oy or oi

oyster

oyster

oil can

oil can

Match the words

Read the words. Colour **oy** or **oi**. Match the words to their meanings.

soil	a Chinese sauce
boiler	money
enjoy	work hard
spoil	part of the ground/outdoors
coins	bothering or getting on your nerves
annoying	it heats water
toil	to like doing something
soy	harm

Match the words

Read the words. Colour **air** or **are**. Match the words to their meanings.

airport	a dummy for scaring away birds
beware	get ready
software	left over
scarecrow	a place where planes take off and land
wheelchair	fix or mend
prepare	watch out
spare	a program for a computer
repair	a seat on wheels to help people get around

Sounds like ur

purse

purse

Earth

Earth

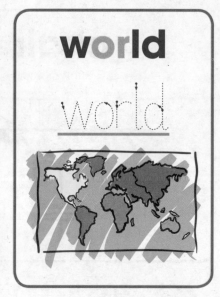

world

world

Read the rhyme

Colour the letters that say **ur**: **ur**   ear   or
See if you can spot another set of letters that
say **ur**! Circle them.

The early bird catches the worm.
Here's a good one – nice and
firm.

To earn a worm I have to be
early.
Here's a nice one – fat and
curly.

Teacher's tip

Begin by reading the rhyme to the learner and asking him/her which
sound they hear often. Ask the learner to write the letters that stand
for the 'ur' sound. Then show the pictures and words at the top of the
page and read them aloud. Point out the different letters that can
be used to write this sound. The learner could then follow the rhyme on
the page as you read it with him/her. Remind the learner of other
sounds: 'er' in German, alert, perm; 'ir' in girl, third, circus. *N.B. 'air' and
'are' represent a different sound but some regional pronunciations may
make them similar.*

Read and match the words

Read the words. Listen to the **ur** sound.
Look at the letters. Colour the letters that say **ur**.

nurse	learn	word	burst
curve	worship	pearl	earn
worth	further	worst	search

Match the words to the ones in the chart.
Write the words below.

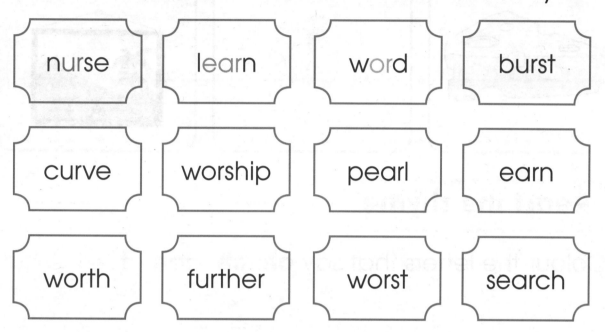

purse	Earth	world

Sounds like ch

cheese

match

picture

Read the rhyme

Colour the letters that say **ch**: **ch** **tch** **t**

The vulture is a greedy creature.

Its bald head is a natural feature.

It sits on a branch to watch for lunch.

Then snatches as much as it can to munch.

Read and match the words

Read the words. Listen to the **ch** sound.
Look at the letters. Colour the letters that say **ch**.

chicken   stitch   nature   fetch

mixture   peach   bench   butcher

capture   teacher   ditch   fracture

Match the words to the ones in the chart.
Write the words below.

🧀 **cheese**	**match**	🖼 **picture**

When le says l

bottle

bottle

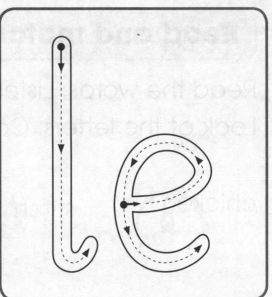

Read the rhyme

Circle **le** in the rhyme.

Mr Noble makes apple crumble

Mrs Noble likes to grumble,

"What a mess on my table! I wish you were able

To make a simple crumble without this jumble.

It's double the trouble when you make a

crumble."

Write the words

Write the **le** words for the pictures. Circle **le** in the words.

kett____

jung____

buck____

pudd____

need____

tab____

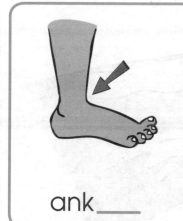

ank____

eag____

puzz____

When st says s

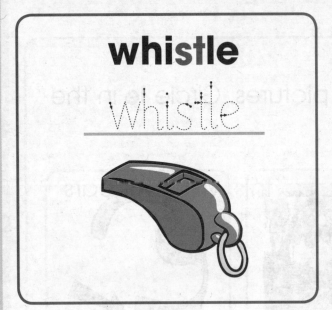

whistle

whistle

Read the rhyme

Circle **st** in the rhyme.

Christmas shopping – jostle and hustle.
Away from the bustle,
Ice and snow glisten.

I listen
To paper rustle.

Match the words

Read the words. Colour **st**. Match the words to their meanings.

bristles	you do this with your ears
thistle	to close with buttons, laces or a zip
castle	a big strong house like a fort
whistle	part of a brush
wrestle	a spiky plant
nestle	to snuggle into a nest
listen	you blow it to make a noise
fasten	to fight in a contest

Sounds like sh

chef

chef

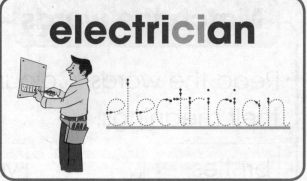

electrician

electrician

station

station

mission

mission

Read the rhyme

Colour the letters that say **sh**: **ch   ci   ti   ssi**

Charlotte the chef waits at the station.
Charlotte the chef is off on vacation.

"Is that your ticket?" asks an official,
"It's not real. It's artificial."

"It's real," says Charlotte with passion.
Charlotte is ready for action.

38

Read and match the words

Read the words. Listen to the **sh** sound.
Look at the letters. Colour the letters that say **sh**.

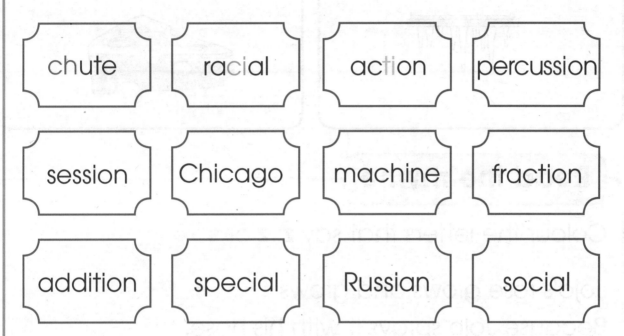

chute	racial	action	percussion
session	Chicago	machine	fraction
addition	special	Russian	social

Match the words to the ones in the chart.
Write the words below.

chef	electrician
station	**mission**

Read the rhyme

Colour the letters that say **z**: **z** or **s**

Jojo's rose grows and grows
Because Jojo sprays it with his hose.

"I'll win a prize
With a rose this size,"
Says Jojo with his nose to the rose.

Teacher's tip

Say some words and names that begin with the 'z' sound. For example, zoo, zoom, zebra, Zakir, zigzag. Ask the learner what sound the words start with and which letter stands for that sound. Explain that in some words 's' can say 'z' (say the sound here, not the letter name), but this is usually where the 'z' sound is not at the beginning of the word, e.g: easy, cause, vase. Tell the learner that there are no other rules about when to use 's' and when to use 'z' – they just have to be learned!

Read and match the words

Read the words. Listen to the **z** sound.
Look at the letters. Colour the letter that says **z**.

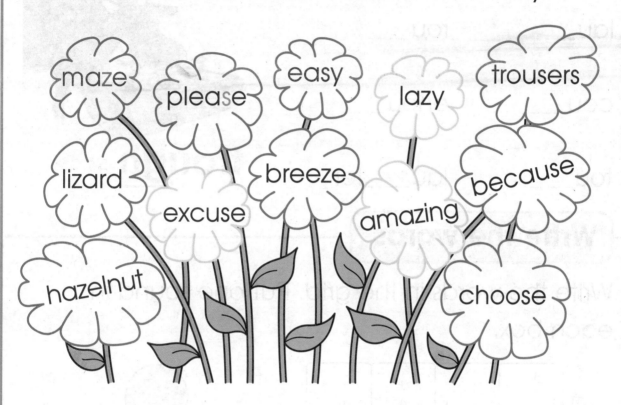

maze   please   easy   lazy   trousers
lizard   breeze   because
excuse   amazing
hazelnut   choose

Match the words to the ones in the chart.
Write the words below.

 **freeze**	 **cheese**

When gh says f

Make the words

Make some words where **gh** says f. Read the words.

lau____   rou____

cou____   enou____

tou____   lau____ter

trough

Write the words

Write the words in the grid. Put one sound in each box.

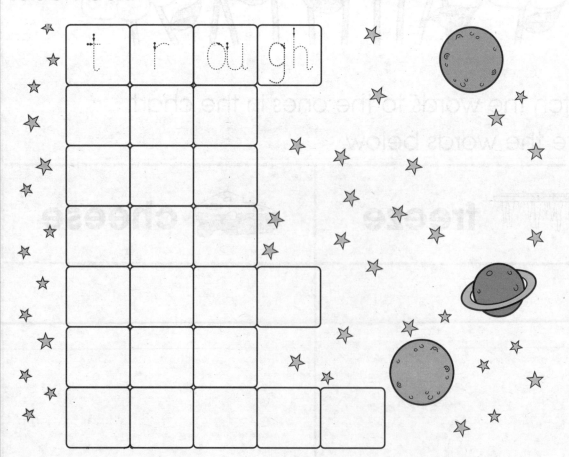

Make the words

Make some words with **sc**. Read the words.

___ene   ___ent   ___ience   mu___le

___issors   cre___ent   ___enery

Write the words

Write one of the words you made in each sentence.

 What a pretty __scene__.

 The _____ery is lovely here.

 Tonight the shape of the moon is

a _____.

 That's a strong _____.

 This _____ smells like roses.

 I am learning _____.

 We use _____ for cutting paper.

Suffix -ed (1)

post → ed

posted

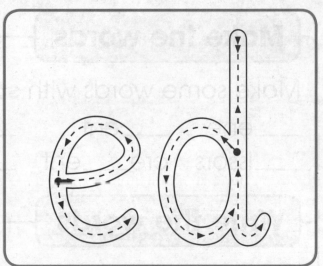

Read the words

Circle **-ed** in the words.

roasted

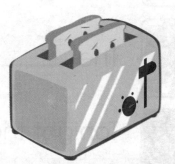

toasted

painted

fainted

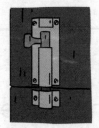

bolted

jolted

Write the words

Add **-ed** to the end of each word.
Write the new word in the gap.

float

Yesterday I _floated_ in the pool.

act

Yesterday I _____ in a play.

boast

Yesterday I _____ about my work.

land

Yesterday I _____ on the moon.

mend

Yesterday I _____ the gate.

splash → ed

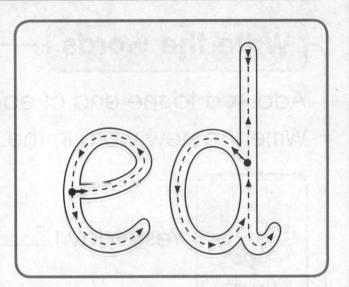

Read the rhyme

Circle **-ed** in the rhyme.

I mixed it.

I fixed it.

I smashed it.

I crashed it.

I rowed it.

I mowed it.

Write the words

Add **-ed** to the end of each word.
Write the new word in the gap.

watch

Yesterday I ___watched___ television.

pick

Yesterday I _____ some flowers.

row

Yesterday I _____ a boat.

jump

Yesterday I _____ over a wall.

help

Yesterday I _____ my mum.

Suffix -ed (3)

knit **+** t → **ed**
knitt → **ed**

knitted

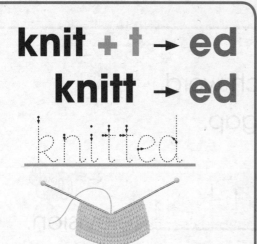

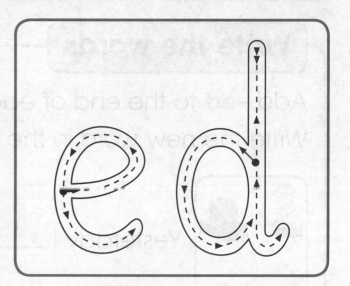

Read the rhyme

Circle **-ed** in the rhyme.

I clipped it.

I snipped it.

I chopped it.

I dropped it.

I clapped.

I flapped.

Write the words

Add **-ed** to the end of each word.
Write the new word in the gap.

slip

Yesterday I _slipped_ on a banana skin.

whip

Yesterday I _____ some cream.

hum

Yesterday I _____ a tune.

hop

Yesterday I _____ along a line.

Suffix -ing (1)

play → ing

playing

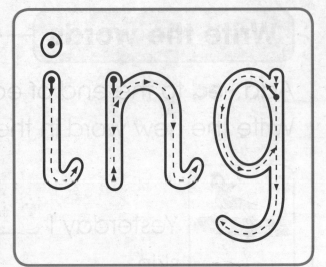

Read the rhyme

Circle **-ing** in the rhyme.

I am rushing,

teeth need brushing,

lolly licking,

football kicking,

hiding, peeping,

now I'm sleeping!

Write the words

Add **-ing** to each word and write it under the picture.

bend	catch	cook	draw	jump
	sing	lift	pull	read

pulling

Suffix -ing (2)

ride → ing
rid → ing

riding

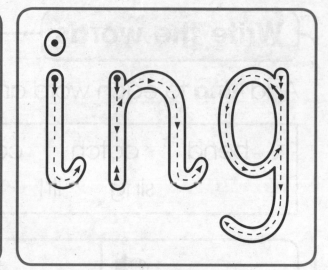

Read the words

Circle **-ing** in the words.

wave – waving

shave – shaving

hide – hiding

slide – sliding

hose – hosing

close – closing

Add -ing

Do these word sums with **-ing**. Remember to take off **e**. Write each word.

| write | + | ing |

writing

| smile | + | ing |

_____

| stroke | + | ing |

_____

| bake | + | ing |

_____

| dive | + | ing |

_____

| bite | + | ing |

_____

Take off -ing

Take **-ing** off each word. Put the **e** back.
Write the new word.

hoping	skating	taking
_____	_____	_____
wiping	joking	using
_____	_____	_____

Suffix -ing (3)

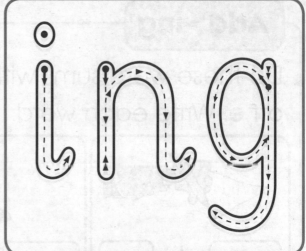

Read the words

Circle **-ing** in the words.

 yap – yapping

 tap – tapping

 pin – pinning

 win – winning

 tug – tugging

 hug – hugging

Write the words

Add **-ing** to each word. Don't forget to double the last letter. Write the new word in the gap.

swim

I like _____.

skip

I like _____.

cut

I like _____.

dig

I like _____.

drum

I like _____.

nod

I like _____.

Suffix –s

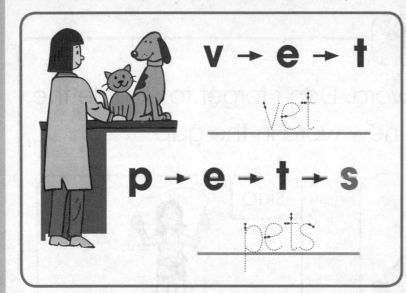

Read the words

Circle **–s** in the words.

One toy, two boys.

One cat, two rats.

One rug, two bugs.

One man, two vans.

Write the words

Write the missing words.

One	Two
One cake	Two cakes
One kite	Two _____
One bone	Two _____
One nail	Two _____
One tree	Two trees
One _____	Two boats
One _____	Two clouds
One _____	Two mugs

Teacher's tip

Read the first example with the learner and ask, 'How do words change when they change from one thing to more than one?' (*Answer: Usually we add 's'.*) Ask the learner to write the missing words and then read the words in the 'two' column aloud. Ask if the 's' at the end always says the same sound. (*Answer: No – sometimes it says 'ss' – as in boats, cakes, kites. At other times it says 'z' – as in mugs, trees, bones, clouds, nails.*)

Suffix -es

glass → es

glass glasses

Read the words

Circle **-es** in the words.

one match

two matches

one patch

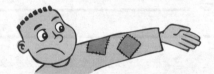

two patches

one box

two boxes

one fox

a family of foxes!

Write the words

Write the missing words.

One	Two
one brush	two _____
one box	two _____
one branch	two _____
one watch	two _____
one _____	two dishes
one _____	two peaches
one _____	two arches
one _____	two sixes

Teacher's tip

Remind the learner how words change when they change from one thing to more than one. (*Reminder: Usually we add 's'.*) On a separate piece of paper, write 'wish' and ask the learner to make it say more than one wish. Point out that 'wishs' is difficult to say, so words like this have 'es' added. After completing the page you could challenge the learner to find and list other words that change in the same way. (You could also keep a list and make the challenge to list any words you haven't already thought of!)

fast → er

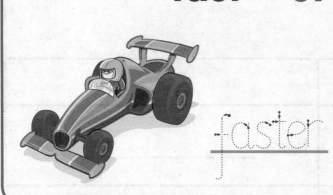

faster

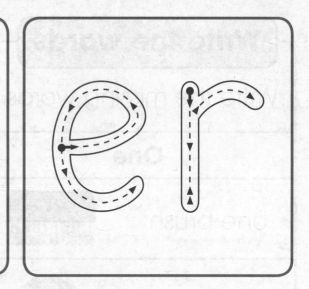

Read the words

Circle **-er** in the words.

I'm getting stronger.

I'm getting longer.

I'm getting taller.

I'm getting smaller.

I'm getting colder.

I'm getting older.

Add -er

Do these word sums with **-er**. Write each word.

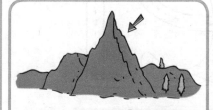

high $+$ er

_____

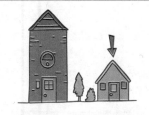

low $+$ er

_____

slow $+$ er

_____

weak $+$ er

_____

new $+$ er

_____

bright $+$ er

_____

Take off -er

Take **-er** off each word. Write the new word.

neater	darker	lighter
_____	_____	_____
cooler	richer	poorer
_____	_____	_____

Suffix -er (2)

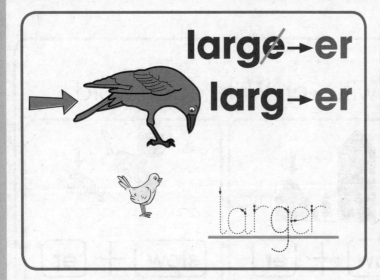

large~~e~~ → er
larg → er

larger

Read the words

Circle **-er** in the words.

gentle → gentler

loose → looser

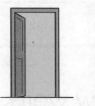

wide → wider

ripe → riper

white → whiter

late → later

Add -er

Add **-er** to these words. Remember to take off **e**.
Write the new words.

fine _____   nice _____

brave _____   tame _____

simple _____   rare _____

Take off -er

Take **-er** off each word. Put the **e** back.
Write the new word.

later	wider	looser
_____	_____	_____

safer	fiercer	nicer
_____	_____	_____

Suffix –er (3)

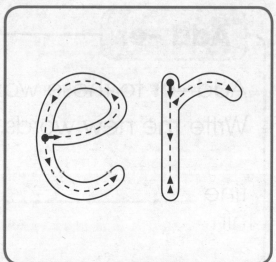

Read the words

Circle **-er** in the words.

getting wetter

getting hotter

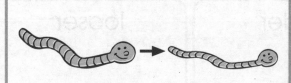

getting thinner

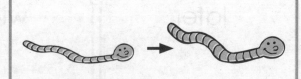

getting fatter

getting fitter

getting sadder

Add -er

Add **-er** to these words. Remember to double the last letter.
Write the new words.

thin _____   flat _____

dim _____   mad _____

hot _____   trim _____

Take off -er

Take **-er** off each word. Don't forget to take off the letter that was doubled.
Write the new word.

bigger	wetter	hotter
_____	_____	_____

fatter	fitter	sadder
_____	_____	_____

Suffix –est (1)

 **fast → est**

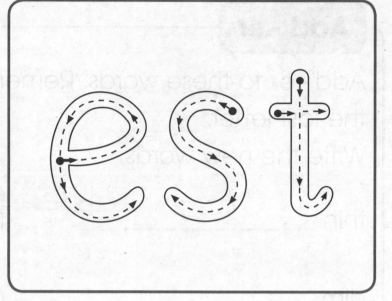

Read the sentences

Read the sentences. Circle **-est** in the words.

I'm the strongest.

I'm the longest.

I'm the tallest.

I'm the smallest

I'm the coldest.

I'm the oldest.

Add -est

Do these word sums with **-est**. Write each word.

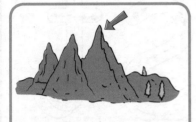

high	+	est

_____

low	+	est

_____

slow	+	est

_____

weak	+	est

_____

new	+	est

_____

bright	+	est

_____

Take off -est

Take **-est** off each word. Write the new word.

neatest	darkest	lightest
_____	_____	_____

coolest	richest	poorest
_____	_____	_____

Suffix –est (2)

large → est
larg → est

largest

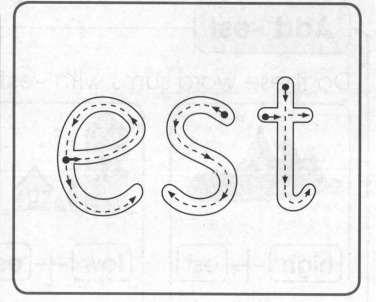

Read the words

Read the words. Circle **-est** in the words.

gentle → gentlest

loose → loosest

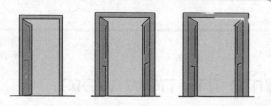

wide → widest

ripe → ripest

white → whitest

late → latest

Add -est

Add **-est** to these words. Remember to take off **e**. Write the new words.

fine _____   nice _____

brave _____   tame _____

simple _____   rare _____

Take off -est

Take **-est** off each word. Don't forget to put the **e** back. Write the new word.

latest	widest	loosest
_____	_____	_____

safest	fiercest	scarcest
_____	_____	_____

Suffix -est (3)

big **+ g** → **est**
bigg → **est**

biggest

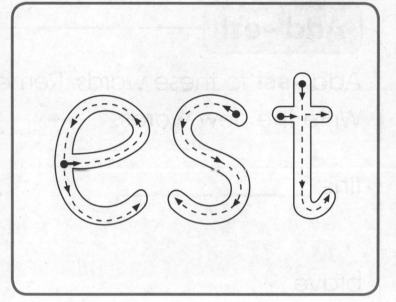

Read the words

Read the words. Circle **-est** in the words.

The wettest day.

The hottest day.

The thinnest worm

The fattest worm.

I'm the fittest.

The dimmest light.

Add -est

Add **-est** to these words. Remember to double the last letter. Write the new words.

thin _____   flat _____

dim _____   mad _____

hot _____   trim _____

Take off -est

Take **-est** off each word. Don't forget to take off the letter that was doubled. Write the new word.

biggest	wettest	hottest
_____	_____	_____

fattest	fittest	saddest
_____	_____	_____

Suffixes

Suffix –ful

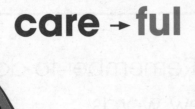

careful

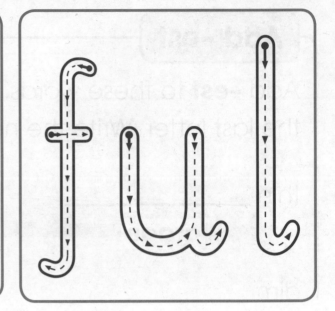

Read the rhyme

Circle **-ful** in the rhyme.

As playful as a kitten.

As useful as a bee.

As powerful as a lion.

As cheerful as me!

72

Write the words

Find the words in the forest. Write the words.
Add **-ful** to the end of each word.

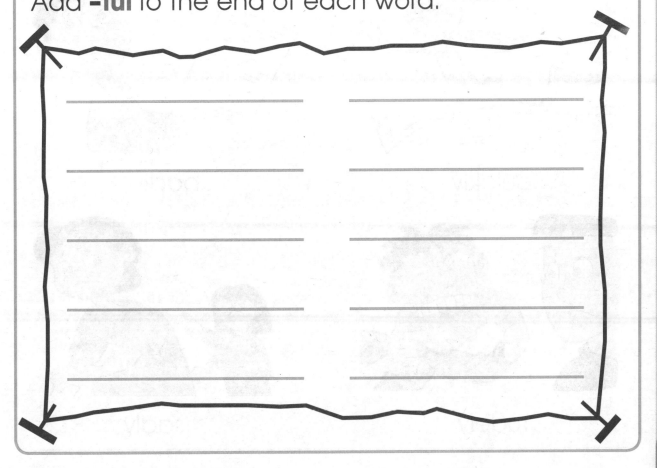

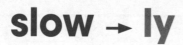

slow → ly

slowly

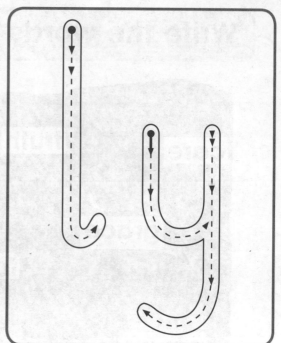

Read the words

Circle **-ly** in the words.

quickly

badly

rudely

sadly

Write the words

Add **-ly** to the words in the boxes.
Write these words in the gaps.
Read the sentences.

bright____	The sun shone _____.
loud____	The lion roared _____.
safe____	I crossed the road _____.
fair____	I played the game _____.
sad____	The girl cried _____.
neat____	I always write _____.
rude____	Some children speak _____.
careful____	I always spell _____.

Suffix -ly (2)

happy + **i** → **ly**
happi → **ly**

happily

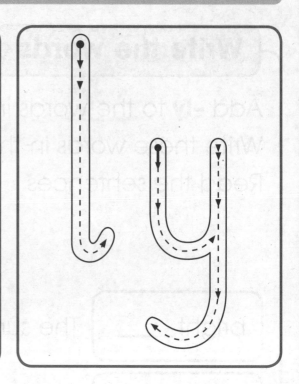

Read the words

Circle **-ly** in the words.

easily

noisily

merrily

angrily

Write the words

Add **-ly** to the words in the boxes.
Remember to change **y** to **i** first.
Write these words in the gaps.
Read the sentences.

cheeky____	The girl spoke to the teacher _____.
nasty____	The boy made fun of me _____.
clumsy____	She knocked over the jug _____.
lucky____	_____ I have a coat with me.
funny____	_____ there were no children at school.
lazy____	The cat stretched _____.
creepy____	The ghost slid into the room _____.
gloomy____	"We're going to lose the match," he said _____.

Suffix -y

snow → y

snowy

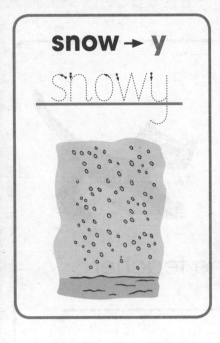

 icé → y

ic → y

icy

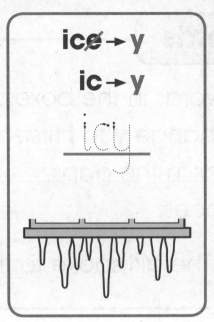

sun + n → y

sunn → y

sunny

Read the words

Read the weather forecast. Circle **-y** in the words.

It will be sunny here and shady there,

Squally, blustery, breezy, blowy – windy everywhere.

Snowy, icy, frosty and chilly

In places where it's hilly.

Hazy, misty, foggy and worst of all – smoggy.

Muddy here and showery there

Thundery, drizzly, choppy at sea – rainy everywhere.

Read and match the words

Read the words. Match the
-y words to the ones in the chart.
Write the **-y** words on the chart.

fizz → fizzy   taste → tasty   wobble → wobbly

spice → spicy   slop → sloppy   crunch → crunchy

chew → chewy   flake → flaky   grease → greasy

run → runny   salt → salty   crackle → crackly

snowy	**icy**	**sunny**

Prefix un-

un → lucky

unlucky

lucky   **unlucky**

Read the rhyme

Circle **un-** in the rhyme.

Pack your case for your holiday.

Unpack your things straight away.

It makes me happy to meet new friends.

But I am unhappy when my holiday ends.

Make the words

Make some words with **un-**.
Read the words you make.

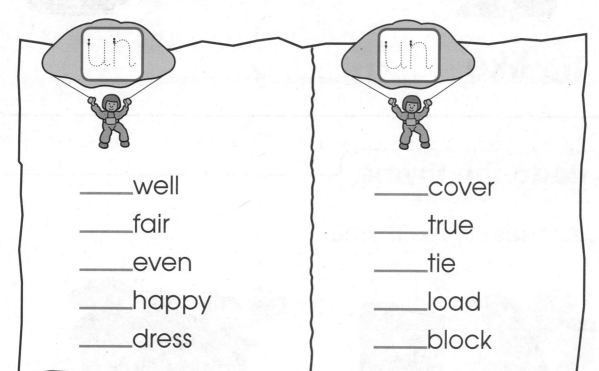

____well

____fair

____even

____happy

____dress

____cover

____true

____tie

____load

____block

Write words

Write the opposite of each word below.

uncover _____cover_____   unhappy _____

unload _____   untie _____

undress _____   untrue _____

unfair _____   unwell _____

unblock _____   uneven _____

Prefix dis-

dis → like

like _dislike_

Read the rhyme

Circle **dis-** in the rhyme.

We are good when we obey

but we're not good when we disobey.

When Mum and Dad appear,

like a flash we disappear!

Make the words

Make some words with **dis-**. Write the words.

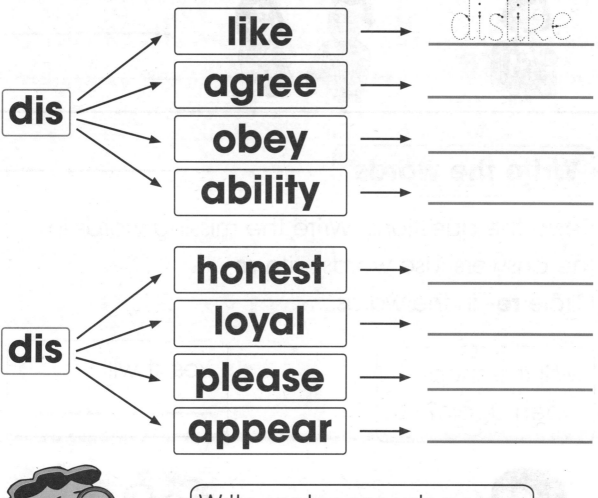

dis → like → <u>dislike</u>

agree → _____

obey → _____

ability → _____

dis → honest → _____

loyal → _____

please → _____

appear → _____

Write sentences using some of the words you made.

_____

_____

_____

Prefix re-

Shall I load the DVD again?

Yes. Please reload it.

re → load

reload

Write the words

Read the questions. Write the missing words in the answers. Use words with **re-**.
Circle **re-** in the words.

Will the shop open again?

Yes, it will
_____.

Shall I play that song again?

Yes, please
_____ it.

Make the words

Make some words with **re-**. Read the words.

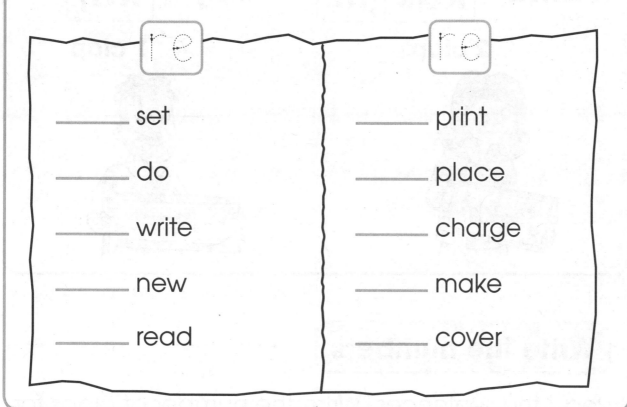

re
_____ set
_____ do
_____ write
_____ new
_____ read

re
_____ print
_____ place
_____ charge
_____ make
_____ cover

Write the words

Write a word that means to do these again:

heat _____   appear _____
make _____   boot _____
check _____   capture _____
count _____   dial _____
fill _____   fold _____

Syllables

The children say their names. They clap for each beat.

Rakhi → | **Rak** | **hi** | **Raj** → | **Raj** |

2 claps   1 clap

Write the numbers

Read the sentences. Write the number of claps for each name.

My name is Asha.	My name is Manohar.
	A	sha			Man	o	har	
I clap _____ claps.	I clap _____ claps.
My name is Christopher.	My name is Sita.
	Chris	to	pher			Si	ta	
I clap _____ claps.	I clap _____ claps.

Match the words

Match the words that have 'look-alike', 'sound alike' spellings.

Read the words.

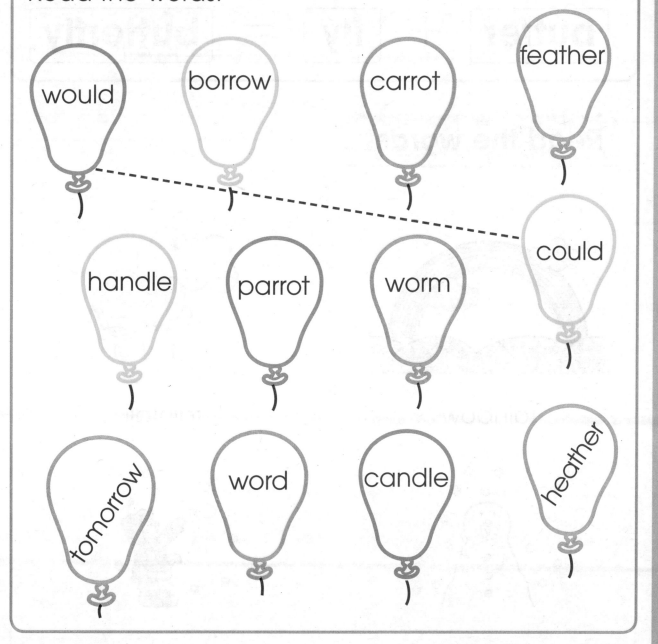

would	borrow	carrot	feather
handle	parrot	worm	could
tomorrow	word	candle	heather

Teacher's tip

Explain that sometimes it helps when spelling a tricky word if you know other words that are like it in some way. Show some examples, e.g:
- treasure/measure ('ea' and 's' might cause problems)
- heart/hearth ('ear' might be a problem)
- danger/ranger, but banger/clanger
- shoe/canoe

Compound words (1)

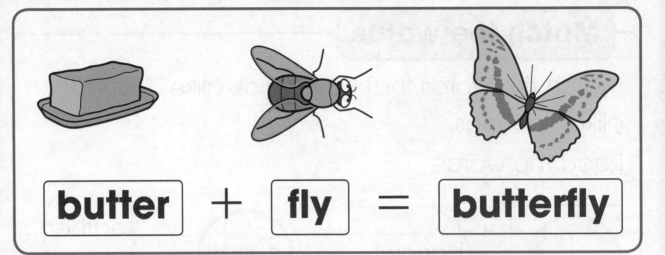

butter + **fly** = **butterfly**

Read the words

rainbow

rainfall

snowman

snowball

Word sums

Do these word sums. Write the answers.

tooth	+	brush	=	_____
bed	+	room	=	_____
wind	+	mill	=	_____
butter	+	cup	=	_____
star	+	light	=	_____
lady	+	bird	=	_____
sheep	+	dog	=	_____
hand	+	bag	=	_____
sun	+	shine	=	_____
book	+	mark	=	_____

Compound words (2)

| horse | + | shoe | = | horseshoe |

Read the rhyme

Worms are found
underground.

Children run around
in the **playground**.

It's nice and bright
in the **sunlight**.

We all sleep tight
in the **moonlight**.

Make the words

Make some compound words. Write the words.

hair	cake	
pan	day	
rain	cloth	
birth	brush →	hairbrush
table	bag	
book	bow	
hand	box	
letter	case	

Clues for tricky words

family

I am in my fam**i**ly.

shoe

The sh**oe** sh**one**.

Read the sentences

Read the sentences.

There's a **g** in the si**g**n.

A **ball**oon is like a **ball**.

10

We of**ten** count to **ten**.

Teacher's tip

Explain that some words have unusual spellings but that it sometimes helps if you use clues to help. Show the examples at the top of the page. It also helps if you learn the words by saying them as they are spelled. For example:

- cup – board
- fri – end
- of – ten (stressing the 'f' sound and the final syllable 'ten')
- sig – n.

This is sometimes called 'spell-speak'.

Write the words

Read the tricky words.
Cover the words. Write the words.

busy	across	friend

The bus is **bus**y.	There's a cross **a**cross the page.	**I** am your friend to the **end**.
	_____	_____
knee	office	cupboard

I bend my **k**nee to **k**ick.	There's **ice** in the off**ice**.	There's a **cup** on the **board** in the **cupboard**.
_____	_____	_____

Remembering tricky words

Write the words

Read the tricky words and clues.
Write the words.

equal **?????** **e**very **q**uestion mark **u**nder **a** **l**ine *equal*	beauty  **b**ig **e**ars **a**re **u**seful **t**o **y**ou
cycle  **c**an **y**ou **c**ircle **l**egs **e**asily	laugh  **l**ook **a**t **u**gly **g**orillas **h**owling

Note to teachers	Some learners might benefit from completing one exercise at a time. Other learners (if they are confident readers) might be able to read an entire page, or even two pages at a time.
	Explain to the learner that the tests will show what he/she has learned. Tell the learner that there will be some words he/she might never have heard before but that they can be sounded using what he/she knows about letters and sounds.
	Explain to the learner what to do. For correct answers, use words such as 'Well done', 'You did well.' If incorrect, praise the learner for having a try: 'It doesn't matter if you get things wrong. That's how we know what you need to practise.'

Read the words and names.

Exercise 1

claim	slate	invite	flight
brewer	hollow	flavour	neighbour
charcoal	palm	honey	saucer

Exercise 2

board	freight	shield	believe
shriek	tomatoes	annoying	quoit
prepare	airline	dearth	world

Exercise 3

earthquake	satchel	hatchet	adventure
mixture	fetching	whistling	scrambled
racial	suction	station	lizard

What have I learned?

Read the words and names.

Exercise 4

enough	muscle	scissors	reported
diluted	tangled	clamped	stripped
treading	amusing	working	stalking

Exercise 5

calming	brewing	escaping	skidding
clutches	porches	birches	stranger
stronger	finer	fiercest	gentlest

Exercise 6

wonderful	awful	colourful	disgraceful
usually	unfairly	clumsily	nastily
unluckily	unwillingly	discovers	disobeyed

Exercise 7

disappearing	dishonest	recover	retrace
reappear	Christopher	featherweight	dragonfly
benchmark	busy	friend	cupboard

The author and publisher are grateful to the copyright holders for permission to use quoted materials and images.

P22 ©Matthew Cole

All other images are are ©iStockphoto/Thinkstock, ©Hemera/Thinkstock, ©Getty images/Dynamic Graphics/liquidlibrary/Thinkstock and Letts Educational, an imprint of HarperCollins*Publishers*

Published by Collins India
A division of HarperCollins*Publishers* India Private Limited
A-75, Sector – 57,
Noida – 201301

**Browse the complete Collins catalogue at
www.collins.in**

First edition 2013
Latest reprinted edition 2017

© HarperCollins*Publishers* India Private Limited 2013

Reprint: 10 9 8 7 6 5 4 3

ISBN-13 978-9-35-136035-3

Typeset by Planman Technologies

Artwork and layout by Planman Technologies

Printed and bound by Saurabh Printers Pvt. Ltd.

MRP: ₹212

How to use this book

The teacher should help the learner work through this book unit by unit because the activities build on what has already been learned.

Learners should work through one or two pages at a time. The teacher should not forget to reward the learner with praise and encouragement.

Before beginning each page the teacher should ensure that the learner knows what the pictures represent. The images should be familiar, but learners have different experiences and might use different words for some of them.

If the learner finds an activity too difficult, stop – the learner needs more practice. For example:
- 'playing with words' (e.g. making up rhymes, especially silly ones!)
- recognising when sounds in words are the same or different
- recognising common spelling patterns in words
- looking for words in everyday print (shop signs, notices, road signs, shop names, instructions)
- helping to read simple instructions for equipment or to make things
- writing greetings cards and letters.

This can be done in everyday situations, for example: reading signs and simple instructions together, pointing out words with similar or unusual spelling patterns – and, of course, reading and enjoying stories and poems.

To help with spelling some difficult words you can use 'spell-speak'. This means pronouncing words as they are spelled. For example:
- pronouncing lis – ten
- pronouncing the 'c' in scissors as 'k' and hissing the ss
- pronouncing cupboard as 'cup – board'.

There is a **What have I learned?** section at the end of the book that can be used for testing what the learner has learned. In this section there are no pictures to use as clues – the learner will use phonic knowledge only to read the words.

Learners from different regions and with different mother tongues will show variations in pronunciation. These should be accepted so long as they do not hinder communication.

Terms used in this book:

blend	Where two or more letters are sounded individually and then blended to read or spell a word.
consonant	The letters of the alphabet that are not **vowels**. Y can be used as either a vowel or a consonant. In English, **consonant phonemes** can be represented by more than one letter, for example: ch, th, sh, ng.
digraph	The two letters representing a single phoneme (sound), e.g. 'ay' in 'play'. These two letters are a grapheme.
grapheme	The letter(s) that represent a **phoneme**. For example, the following graphemes can all represent the same phoneme: i (ibex, silent), y (cry, deny), igh (high, night), ie (cries, tried), i–e (bite, rice).
phoneme	The smallest unit of sound in a word. For example, 'cat' has three phonemes, represented by the letters c, a and t. A phoneme can be represented by two or more letters: f**or**t, h**igh**, n**eigh**.
prefix	An element made up of one or more letters placed at the beginning of a word to change its meaning.
split digraph	The two letters representing a single sound that are separated by another letter, e.g. the a–e in 'make'.
suffix	An element made up of one or more letters placed at the end of a word to change its meaning.
syllable	A unit or portion of a word that is pronounced without interruption, e.g. 'cat' in caterpillar. Caterpillar can be split into four syllables: cat-er-pill-ar. At a simple level, a syllable can be thought of as a 'beat'. Children can 'clap' each syllable.
vowel	The letters a, e, i, o and u. Y can also be used as a vowel, e.g. gym, rely. In English, some vowel **phonemes** are represented by groups of letters: or, ar, oo, igh, eigh.